Take Control c

Self Help for Depression, Anxiety Disorders, Confidence & More

With Holistic Well-Being Coach

Daniel Jones

GHR (Reg.), GQHP, DHypPsych(UK), Dip.I.Hyp.E.Psy.NLP Prac (BHR)

D.NLP, HypPrac, BSYA (B.D, Cur.Hyp, H.Md, Zen.Md) MASC (Relax, NLP)

Contact the author:

www.ericksonian-hypnotherapy.com

Second Edition 2011

Published and Printed By Lulu.com

Copyright © Daniel Jones 2009

ISBN: 978-1-4475-4634-4

Acknowledgements

Thank you to those that have contributed to my lifelong adventures. I have travelled along smooth roads through beautiful lands; and rocky roads through the moonless dark of the night. I have climbed mountains wondering when I will reach the top and what I will discover. I have travelled through darkness and discovered light; and travelled through light before discovering darkness. I have given a gift to everyone I have met; and have been privileged to receive a gift from each person in return.

It is only from all of these experiences and interactions that I am able to write this book. Every experience is a developmental opportunity to learn from so thank you to all those people.

Contents

Introduction

For over eighteen years I have helped people to help themselves with a wide variety of problems from depression and anxiety to performance enhancement and personal development.

When I decided to write this book I didn't want to write just another self help book; I wanted to write something that would be easy to read; quick to read and something that is actually useful. The book had to be reader friendly.

Over the years I have read my fair share of self help and performance development books. Each one contains a nugget of usefulness yet often only focuses on one area of a person's life like achieving business success, beating anxiety, overcoming depression.

I wanted to write something that people would pick up and read and re-read if they have a different problem in the future, and would lend the book to friends and family or read bits of the book to see how to help those friends and family.

This book is designed to be something that will be a useful part of your life not just a few hours read. I wanted to create something that covered many of life's difficulties so that over the years you always have a reference manual with ruffled edges from continued use.

Unlike many other books I don't want to portray that I am the cause of your positive change. My aim is to be a guide that gives you ideas to help you take control in your life for your own change work. I always aim to empower my clients and those I meet throughout my life not to make the changes for my clients.

Basic Emotional Needs

We all have basic emotional needs that need to be met. With each of us the level they need to be met at is set differently. For example some people need a lot of attention, others need a little attention.

Many emotional problems occur due to one or more of our needs not being met to our satisfaction. It could be that we are getting too much of the need or too little.

From reading about the needs most people intuitively know which needs are being meet appropriately and which aren't.

The main categories of basic emotional needs are:

- **To give and receive attention** (e.g., socialising)

- **The mind body connection** (e.g., not sleeping can lower the immune system)

- **To have purpose and goals** (e.g., having an aim in life)

- **Belonging to a wider community** (e.g., joining a group or a religion)

- **The need for stimulation and creativity** (e.g., working at achieving your goals)

- **The need to feel understood and emotionally connected to others** (e.g., having a close group of friends, having a loving partner)

- **The need to feel a sense of control & independence** (e.g., knowing what is in your control & making decisions)

- **To feel a sense of security** (e.g., financially, within a relationship)

- **Having a sense of status within a social group** (e.g., holding a specific position in a company)

- **Having a sense of competence & achievement** (e.g., being good at your job, meeting your targets/goals)

(Adapted from the book 'Human Givens' by Joe Griffin & Ivan Tyrrell)

These are some of the main emotional needs that need to be met to ensure a healthy balanced life. You can look down the list and see if these needs are being met adequately in your life. Problems usually occur when any need or essential skill (see essential skills chapter) isn't being met adequately or appropriately.

For example it could be getting a migraine to gain attention. Or getting an addiction that tricks you into believing it gives you a sense of control. Or joining a gang and getting into the gang's culture to feel understood and connected.

Over the next few pages we will look at these basic needs in turn and what you can do if any 'need' isn't being met.

To give and receive attention

It is important that you feel you give others an appropriate level of attention and that you receive a level of attention that you are also comfortable with.

If you don't feel you give or receive enough attention take some time to plan/write down/or work out with a friend how you can get attention. It could be that you decide to take up a leisure activity, or you find a way to socialise whether this is going out with friends or having friends round for a meal.

By putting some time and effort into getting this need met you should notice the changes within just a few weeks or months and many people notice much sooner.

The Mind Body Connection

For optimum mental and physical wellbeing you can begin to pay attention to your mind body connection.

Each day you go through an energy cycle of highs and lows (Ultradian Rhythm). This cycle takes about 90 minute where energy gradually increases for the first half of the cycle, and then begins to drop off through the second half of the cycle reaching a low point where your mind wants to wander. It is at this point that most people suffer with cravings (if they have an addiction) where the mind is trying to make the person take a break and rest for about 15-20 minutes. It is important that you take a break at these times to allow your mind and body to recharge. These breaks are like a computer document auto-saving. If you skip them there is more chance of losing information and running at a slower less efficient speed.

If someone has a craving they should use the craving as a sign they should stop and take a break. Then go and sit quietly somewhere. Have a drink of water or juice and relax for about 15 minutes. Some effective ways to relax are to just close your eyes and focus on your breathing, breathing in counting to 7 and out counting to 11, or listening to a brief relaxation track.

This will usually curb most cravings and begin to break the habitual response to act on the craving whilst at the same time improving your energy throughout the day and your sleep at night, also reducing levels of stress and anger and increasing your immune system and health.

To have purpose and goals

If you are lacking purpose in your life you are likely to drift along never quite feeling satisfied.

One way to establish a purpose is to set goals. Not just in work but in your life as a whole. An idea you can use is to get a pen and pad, then close your eyes and relax a moment. After you have begun to start relaxing begin to focus on what you would like your life to be like a year in the future. Get a sense of home life, work life, leisure life. The more vividly you imagine this ideal future the more effective this will be (and you can do this often). Then open your eyes and write down at the bottom (or over to the right if the paper is landscape) in detail that future life. What you will see, hear, feel. What you will be doing, the effect this will have on those around you etc. Then write for each aspect of that future what you have to do just before that can become reality, and then just before that etc until you are back in the present. You should then have stages for each goal from the first step you need to take in the present to that future. Next close your eyes and imagine going through all of those stages into the future. Imagine the next year's worth of events. Notice more and more detail each time you do this. Actively look out for more detail.

When you go to bed; before you go to sleep; run through this process in your mind. Then take action and begin carrying out the first stages. Make the images in your mind compelling; usually this involves making them bright and vivid. Your unconscious mind will also begin to look out for opportunities that will make your dreams a reality.

There was research done where they had a group of people that believed they were failures and unlucky and a group that believed they were successful and lucky. They walked the same route being observed. There was a £10 on the pavement. All of the people that believed they were successes saw the note and picked it up. All the people that believed they were failures didn't see the note. Both groups of people had the same opportunity available to them but their focus determined whether they would take it or not.

Belonging to a wider community

Everybody has a need to feel that they belong to the wider community. They have a need to belong within society. Many people do this by following fashion trends, sharing interests that are acceptable within the wider community (like discussing specific TV programmes) or being a part of a religion or a group.

Some people find their need for belonging to the wider community being over met. They will find that they get too engrossed in a religion or playing a part within a group, or feeling a NEED to HAVE to follow fashion. They can find that it begins to run their life. These people will often end up suffering from anxiety problems which can lead to getting depressed if they feel the pressure to fit in gets on top of them or leads to other problems like debt or putting their need to belong above other important areas of their life.

Others find this need isn't met enough. They find that they get depressed or anxious because they don't feel that they belong. The ideal situation is to be somewhere in between. We all need to belong; while at the same time we all need to be individual. We all need to find the balance that is right for us.

The need for stimulation and creativity

Each of us needs to get appropriate levels of stimulation and creativity. Again as humans we are hardwired with a need for stimulation and creativity, if this is denied it is likely to lead to boredom, anxiety and stress. Without stimulation and creativity boredom can set in and to meet this need people can begin drinking lots of tea or coffee, or smoking more than normal to try to get some stimulation of any kind.

Ideally this need will be met by having opportunities in work to be creative and enough variety for this to be stimulating. Likewise in our everyday personal life we need to have opportunities to be creative and stimulated. This could be based on activities we choose to do, or even taking the decision to redecorate or plan for a party, or going shopping for clothes and imagining different combinations of outfits.

It could be that to get stimulation you take regular holidays to places you've never been before or regularly try new activities or new foods, or create opportunities to give yourself new experiences or even just taking a different route to work.

The need to feel understood and emotionally connected to others

We all have a need to feel connected with others on an emotional level. Usually this can take the form of close relationships with a partner or with a small group of friends.

Often without this need being met people feel alone, even if they have a large circle of friends. People can feel that they KNOW lots of people but no-one understands them. Some people can find that if they start going through an emotionally challenging time they decide to avoid people by spending more and more time alone rather than having a close circle of friends or a loving partner that they can work through their problem with.

The need to feel a sense of control and independence

We all want to have a sense of control in our lives. We want to feel that we have control over what we do in work and what decisions we make. When people don't have a sense of control it can lead to depression, anxiety and feeling helpless. Problems can also occur if you try to have too much control or independence.

Without control people can often turn to ritualistic behaviours or habits as a way of gaining control. If people feel they don't have control in their external lives they often look internally to get control. Many prisoners of war create internal control during torture for example by counting to ten before screaming.

It is important to know what is really in your control and what isn't. When you are able to relax with uncertainty it can make many situations easier to manage and improve your chances of maintaining positive mental health. When control is taken away; people can get angry or frustrated with the cause of that lack of control; and it can feel very disempowering.

The same applies to independence. You want to have just the right amount of independence. Too much and you may feel overwhelmed and alone in times of need.

Not having enough independence can limit growth. Young people often find this. They need a level of independence to grow and develop and learn to become their own person. While parents often want to have control over their son or daughter to keep them safe; this can lead to limiting their developmental opportunities.

When we don't have enough independence we can feel trapped. We may want to free ourselves from this feeling. It is all about finding the balance that is right for us; this can change over time and from situation to situation.

To feel a sense of security

From the moment we are born we look for a sense of security. We want to know that our parents will be there for us. If we hurt ourselves we want a parent to come and help us. If we are hungry we want to know we will get food.

As we grow up we continue to want security physically, environmentally and emotionally. Many people want to have at least one close relationship. We want relationships that are secure and steady, we want financial security and job or career security.

When we don't have security; for example; if we are unsure of our position at work or unsure how safe our job is, or if we have money worries that could lead to losing a house; then we can easily become irritable, short tempered or have panic attacks or depression as the natural instinct is to fight or get anxious to escape the threat.

Essential Skills

As with the 'Basic needs' (see basic needs) there are essential skills that are useful for having a healthy balanced life. As a therapist sometimes I need to teach people certain essential skills just like I sometimes have to help people find ways to get their needs met appropriately. Everyone is born with these essential skills, but through our different upbringings some people are naturally more able to use these skills than others.

- Tolerating uncertainty

- Using critical thinking

- Relaxing

- Using our natural resources

- Managing attention

- Being able to imagine not having the problem

- Objectively viewing problems in your mind

- Imagination and holding different viewpoints

- Learning and remembering

- The ability to communicate effectively

(Adapted from the book 'Human Givens' by Joe Griffin & Ivan Tyrrell)

Many psychological problems arise out of not using these essential skills effectively.

For example smoking to relax, or getting angry because you can't manage your attention effectively or feeling no-one listens to you (needing to work on communication), or getting more depressed because you can't ever believe you will get better, or worrying (misusing the imagination).

Tolerate Uncertainty

Life is full of uncertainty. Managing this uncertainty can be difficult for some people. Many people like things to be clear; they like to know what is expected of them. They like a limited number of choices.

One way of learning to manage uncertainty is to learn how to relax. That way in uncertain situations you can relax and then view the options with a calm frame of mind. The uncertainty is enough to have to deal with without also having to deal with feeling anxious.

Using Critical Thinking

We all have a part of us that logically looks at and analyses situations. In high states of emotion this part of our mind often shuts down to allow for instinctive 'reactive' responses to occur.

By learning to relax you can begin to reduce the increased levels of emotion and objectively view a situation. It could be that you begin to feel anxious in a situation and so take a few deep breaths to calm yourself as you think about what could be causing you to feel anxious and look at the 'reality' of the situation. Or maybe you frequently fall into the same negative habitual patterns and use your critical thinking to explore this and see what you can learn about yourself that can help you to move beyond these old unconscious responses.

Relaxing

As you have probably gathered relaxation is an important skill to have. By learning to relax you can take back control of your mind and begin to master your emotional reactions.

There is nothing wrong with having emotional reactions. In some cases unfortunately those reactions can become unhealthy. For example if someone close to you passes away you are very likely to grieve. This is a natural and healthy part of dealing with loss. If you are still grieving to the same extent a year or two later this may well now be causing other life problems. Or if someone attacks you and you get angry to protect yourself or others or anxious to make you run away this is natural. If because of this incident you now get angry or anxious in many different situations in life that loosely resemble that initial incident then this may have a negative impact on your life and may be a problem. Again if it was a traumatic incident it is natural for the situation to affect you for a while afterwards by perhaps making you wary in situations or respond with anger or anxiety for a while but if it continues for a prolonged period it is likely to begin to become a problem.

By learning to relax you can begin to alter the brain. Every time you recall a memory it gets altered depending on a variety of factors. If for example you are depressed and you recall a happy memory people often think 'I thought I was happy then but I wasn't really that happy' and they take some of the happiness out of the memory. If they think of an upsetting memory whilst feeling happy they don't see the memory as being so upsetting.

This works with anxious or angry memories. If you are relaxed and recall an anxious or angry memory it dilutes it. Or if you are in a situation that may well make you angry or anxious and you relax it reduces the chances of anxiety or anger developing and also reduces the long term emotional impact the situation is likely to have on you.

Using Natural Resources

We all have natural resources and resources from our personal experience of life. One trick to emotional wellbeing is to be able to take a resource from one area of our life and apply it to another.

It could be that you are a master of calm focused attention in business meetings; or can manage hostile situations calmly in work but once you are home with the children you find yourself shouting and getting angry with them.

This kind of situation is a common one. People often have the skills and abilities they need but don't realise it. In this example the parent could look at the process they go through to remain calm and focused at work, what thinking do they do, how do they act, what do they say to themselves in their mind, how do they breathe, what is their body language, what is their mindset before they are in the situation and how do they move on or manage after the situation. They could look at asking themselves these types of questions and then initially practice in their mind using the same processes in situations with their children before then using the same processes in reality with their children.

Managing Attention

Without being able to hold your focus on a task people are unlikely to complete things. We can all manage attention. I have worked over the years with hundreds of children 'diagnosed' with Attention Deficit Hyperactivity Disorder (ADHD) and many of these children allegedly couldn't focus or manage their attention for more than a few minutes.

What I found was that all of them could focus and manage their attention. If they were very engrossed in a subject or something they were doing they would be focusing and managing their attention for 30 minutes or an hour, sometimes even longer. If they were taught or helped to break things down into small manageable chunks they could manage their attention as they were just focusing on one thing for a few minutes before having to focus on the next thing/chunk.

This is often the trick. To break things down into chunks that are just right for how you as an individual manages your attention. You can improve your attention span by gradually increasing the size of the chunks.

By using small chunks it helps tasks to feel more manageable. I made a collection of over 2000 audio clips that could be used by people to create their own self hypnosis tracks.

To do this I had to break it down into manageable targets. To record the audio I focused on creating 200 audio clips before stopping. This was enough for me to be stretched but not so much that I would lose motivation and give up. When I came to name each of the 2000+ files this involved listening to each file and naming each track based on what I said on the track. As this was a long and time consuming task I decided on a target of naming 100 tracks before stopping. Again this was a large enough chunk to stretch me but not so large that I would feel overwhelmed and give up. The final stage was to put all the named tracks into categories to make it easier for the user to find what they may be looking for. For this stage I had to decide what folders to create and then with each of the 2000+ audio clips I had to decide which folder each clip should go under. The target I set myself for this was to organise 100 clips before stopping.

Notice I also broke down the process of creating the product into stages/chunks. The 'creating the audio clips stage', 'naming the clips stage', 'organising the clips stage'.

Everyone has their own strategies that work for them to help them manage attention. As with the 'Using Natural Resources' you can think about times you naturally manage your attention very well and explore what it is about those situations that makes managing your attention easy. The common time people usually manage their attention well is when they are having fun or engrossed in something they enjoy. Also times when you weren't really paying attention or 'trying' you were just 'doing something'.

Imagine Not Having the Problem

When people are stuck in the middle of their personal situation it can be difficult to honestly imagine life being different and the problem not existing. Sometimes circumstances may not change but the way you think about those circumstances can change.

It is very difficult to be motivated to do what is necessary to move on from a situation if the thinking in your mind is that you can't imagine things every being any different regardless of how much you wish they were.

Often this can be helped by relaxing so that you can view the situation more objectively. It can also help to think outside the box a little and think about someone that is in a similar situation that doesn't find it a problem, or someone that has been in a similar situation that overcame it. Or even thinking about what someone else that you know would be able to move on from that problem would do if they were in your situation.

You can also look at what life would be like if the problem wasn't there or wasn't a problem to you. What would you see, hear, feel? What would other people see, hear, feel? How would things be if the problem had never arisen? So you aren't immediately saying you can imagine not having the problem, you're just wondering what life would be like if somehow magically the problem disappeared, wasn't there or was no longer a problem.

This can be a good way of gathering information about possible ways forward from the problem. When I ask people what they would like from therapy they often respond by telling me what they wouldn't like. 'I don't want to smoke', 'I don't want them to kick off all the time', 'I don't want to be fat', 'I don't want to have this fear'.

People rarely tell me what they want instead of the old problem and when I ask them what they want instead they normally reply by telling me they had never really thought about it.

Frequently this has been the main reason they haven't moved on previously because they had never worked out where to move on to.

Imagining and Holding Different Viewpoints

A real skill is the ability to look at situations and think about what other meanings could be there. For example if a child is misbehaving the parent may think they are just being naughty, or they may think 'they are just doing that to annoy me' or they could look at the situation and think about other meanings that may be equally as valid but things that they have control over changing, like 'they are doing that because they want attention' or 'they are misbehaving in class because they are trying to get sent out rather than have to try to do the work that they find difficult as they don't want to look stupid in front of the others in the class'

Depression

Irish Psychologist Joseph Griffin (co-founder of Human Givens Therapy) researched why depressed people dream more than non-depressed people do, and why they always wake up tired. His results led to a greater understanding of depression allowing for quicker treatment. (See 'Human Givens' by Joe Griffin & Ivan Tyrrell)

When someone is depressed they worry regularly throughout the day. Each time they worry they set off a pattern that often doesn't get closed.

For example: worrying what people think or what if this happens etc. All these open patterns need closing that night which causes over dreaming due to the increased number of patterns that have been opened. Because so much of the night is spent dreaming which is about as exhausting as being fully awake, and missing out on deep recuperative sleep the brain wakes the depressed person early to stop them dreaming. They then feel exhausted due to the lack of deep sleep.

Excessive dreaming also stops serotonin production, which leads to feeling low and unmotivated. It also continually fires off the reorientation response (the part of your brain that makes you focus on one thing at a time) which adds to the low motivation as the response stops working effectively at focusing attention and motivating the depressed person. Once the depressed person spends one day with significantly reduced worrying they usually sleep properly that night and feel immediately much better and more able to cope the next day.

Research has shown that in almost all cases depression is not a biological or genetic illness. The biological changes that occur are the result of the depression not the cause. In some cases the biological effects are caused by diet, pregnancy or menopause or some illnesses. Likewise brain damage or a tumour could lead to psychological difficulties like depression.

Genetically there is research in the field of Epigenetics that may show that life situations of previous generations can create epigenetic changes which can be passed on to future generations making them more susceptible to depression or anxiety problems. Research into epigenetics is also pointing at the possibility of being able to 'undo' these changes during your lifetime. So if a mother was in a highly stressful situation during pregnancy and she passed on epigenetic changes which meant the child was more likely to get anxious or angry quickly that child can learn how to relax and how to think about things in a different way and as they begin to master this their life experiences create epigenetic changes undoing the old 'natural' response.

Studies carried out showed that to quickly lift depression what was needed was a mixture of cognitive, behavioural and interpersonal therapies. This has now been improved upon by also utilising a solution-focused approach and a human givens approach.

To help yourself to overcome a period of depression ensure your basic needs are being met and get your focus of attention off of worrying and ruminating and onto problem solving and relaxing the mind. When you do this you increase the chances of the depression lifting quickly.

Most depression is caused by worrying.

It could be worrying about a past problem or event, present problem or event or a future problem or event. This worrying causes over dreaming at night. When you dream too much it inhibits the release of serotonin and is almost as active as being awake. It also reduces the abilities of the immune system. All of this leads to waking up early as your brain wants to stop you from dreaming excessively, then often managing to get back to sleep yet still waking tired and unmotivated. This then starts off the next days' cycle of worrying.

When depressed your thinking style changes as you are in a highly emotional state of mind. It can be like walking around in a trance. You start thinking that everything has always been bad and always will be and that if anything good ever happens it won't last. Because you are in a highly emotional state you can't think effectively about your problems so they can seem easily overwhelming.

As well as making sure your basic needs are being met appropriately and changing your focus to focusing on positives and problem solving to lift depression you can learn to relax. Relaxation leads to a clearer mind allowing you to make better decisions and be more aware of what options are available to you. One of the best ways to relax is to do 7-11 breathing which is where you breathe in deeply to the count of 7 then out to the count of 11. By doing this with the out breath longer than the in breath you trigger the relaxation response. Just 3 or 4 deep 7-11 breaths will help to relax you and focus your mind.

Others ways to relax could be learning a relaxation process like focusing on each body part whilst lying down. You could either tense each body part with an in breath and then release that tension with an out breath or you could just focus on each body part with and in breath and an out breath. You could do this every morning and evening. Or you could take up a relaxing hobby or learn meditation or self hypnosis.

To best challenge your thinking about what it is that you are worrying about and problem solving it. Spend time each morning closing your eyes and truly imagining some good things about the upcoming day. At night or in the evening also take a few moments to imagine what it will be like to feel much better, who will be the first to notice? How will they know? What will your behaviour be like? Really imagine it and feel it. What will your internal dialogue be like?

You can also keep a diary or journal. Writing down three things that went well for you the day before, three things you've got to look forward to today and three things you've got to look forward to in the future. Any problems that arise throughout the day you can write down and then write down a few ideas about how you can resolve that problem or what would have to happen to resolve the problem and what can you do towards moving beyond the problem.

If there is no resolution to the problem or nothing in your control you can look at whether you have any influence over those that do have control about the problem and what that influence is. For example if someone's job is uncertain they may not make the decision over whether they will keep their job or not but may be able to do certain things that will demonstrate to the decision maker that they should keep their job. If you don't have influence or control then you can write down how you would like to handle the situation; how you would like to think about things and what you would have to do or say to yourself to handle things in this new way.

Anxiety

Anxiety is the natural survival response to run or escape a situation being triggered at the wrong time. This response is designed to help you but in modern times this is often triggered by events from job interviews to social situations etc…

Anxiety and panic attacks are caused by a misuse of the imagination. For example worrying about an upcoming presentation you will be giving. Each time you imagine how bad it will go you create a template that your mind follows that tells it how it should feel about that event. Because you have the ability to use your imagination well enough to affect you, this means if you imagine it going well and look forward to it; then that is the template that you lay down. This works by really building up the experience vividly in your mind getting pleasant, desirable feelings linked to the event.

People that have the ability to make themselves feel anxious are in a wonderful and privileged position that many others don't have. Most people struggle to imagine things enough to create an emotional response either positively or negatively. Yet this is exactly the skill that people who can make themselves anxious have. Often this skill is used just to create anxiety because the person isn't consciously controlling what is happening. It's like a TV being on a random channel that happens to be full of scary films but not realising you can use the remote to change channels.

As soon as you realise you can change channels you can change how you feel. If you can make yourself feel anxious you have the skill to make yourself feel calm, or excited, or any other emotion you would like. All it takes is practice to take control of your mind.

Some people say they can't imagine situations going well because they don't believe that it will. The advantage you have by imagining things going well is that it is all in your mind. In your mind you can fly even though you know in reality you can't. So even if you think in reality something would be impossible, in your mind it isn't.

The wonderful thing about imagining things going well in your mind is that you don't have to believe it is going to make any difference. All you have to do is at the time you imagine it going well become absorbed in the experience of everything going well 'as if' it is current reality. Suspend your views or opinions about the 'real future situations' for now.

When you practice something going well in your mind often enough it begins to become a part of you and begins to influence the real world. In your mind you want to see, hear and feel things going well.

When you have panic attacks or get anxious it shuts down the digestive system and all non-essential systems. It prepares your body to fight, run or freeze (playing dead). These responses could save your life in the appropriate situations. Even if it feels like you are going to die, *you won't*. The feelings are because of the digestive system shutting down and because of the adrenaline released into the body. Most people say it feels like butterflies in their stomach, or a churning sensation.

Some people believe they will collapse or faint. Even if you do pass out your breathing will go back to normal and you will come round again. If you have a panic attack, rate the anxiety on a scale out of 10 and you can keep track of how quickly it is going. The chemicals released into the body that cause the feelings of anxiety leave the body after only a short while.

Whenever you are feeling stressed or anxious or just want to relax give 7 – 11 breathing a go. Breathe in to the count of 7 then out to the count of 11.

If you get anxious or have a panic attack remember the **AWARE** technique:

A = **Accept the anxiety**, don't fight it

W= **Watch your anxiety**, rate it from 1-10 and watch as that rating changes

A = **Act with the anxiety**, behave normally & do what you intended to do, breathe normally or do 7-11 breathing

R = **Repeat** all of the above steps until it goes down to an comfortable level

E = **Expect the best**, what you fear most normally never happens, mentally rehearse experiences where you thought you might have felt anxious in the past but surprise yourself when you don't.

Close your eyes, relax, vividly imagine watching yourself remaining calm whilst doing something in the future you would usually have found caused anxiety. Then imagine being in that scene and notice how pleasant it feels to have this different response. Rehearse this regularly.

During a panic attack control your breathing, if you feel it coming you could chew some gum or eat a small amount of food as you can't be anxious at the same time as having your digestive system working.

You can also find time to sit down and relax (perhaps by using self-hypnosis, or by imagining a pleasant scene in your mind, or just by listening to relaxing music) and as you do bring your thumb and forefinger together linking this relaxation feeling to the touching of the thumb and forefinger. Make it so that each time you bring the thumb and forefinger together you remind yourself of the relaxation. This response can then be triggered when you are in a situation that makes you feel anxious. You can practice this 'anchoring' and firing the relaxation response, imagining being in situations that would normally cause anxiety and using the 'anchor' to relax yourself. The more you practice this the stronger the response will be.

Post Traumatic Stress Disorder (PTSD), Fears & Phobias

The process that creates fears, phobias and post-traumatic stress disorder (PTSD) is designed to protect you from harm. It can be a form of one time learning. You can experience an event once (like having a spider, jump on you as a child) and if the emotion of fear (or other strong negative feeling) is strong enough that is all it takes to create a phobia. The same as PTSD – you only have to be involved in one scary car crash to be traumatised by it for life (getting flashbacks etc...)

This process works by being very general, linking a highly emotional event with the environmental stimuli present at the time. This then allows those stimuli to trigger the same high emotion in the future. For example if you got bad news whilst at a party you may have seen balloons at the time so you may get a phobia of balloons. Or if a mugger wore a black shirt when they mugged you, you may get a phobia for black shirts or even for black. The same process causes fetishes. For example, having sex on the floor by some wellington boots and the high emotion gets linked to the sight of the boots then after that you get aroused by the sight of wellington boots.

There is a technique you can use called the rewind technique that a well-trained therapist can do with you. It involves viewing the traumatic memory as if on a TV screen from before the 'scary' part began and through to after the 'scary' part ends. You start by relaxing, creating a 'special calm place' in your mind. Then watching 'you' sitting in a chair watching the screen as that 'you' watches the memory through to the end. Then drifting into the 'you' in the screen and rewinding through the experience really fast back to the beginning before the event began, seeing everything going backwards, hearing everything going backwards. Then drifting out of the screen to the 'you' on the seat, relaxing deeply into this position and watching the old memory in very fast forward to the end. Then again drifting and relaxing into the 'you' in the screen at the end of that old memory and experiencing it in rewind again even faster this time. Then drifting and relaxing back into the 'you' in the chair and watching the memory in even faster fast forward. This process is repeated until the memory can be experienced comfortably.

If there is more than one memory that needs this process then it can be done on all the relevant memories. For example: in cases of abuse or bullying. Usually it only needs to be done on one to three memories. After this if necessary you can imagine vividly, future times when you may be in similar situations and notice how relaxed you can remain. If it makes it easier you can put this memory on a scale of 1-10 and then if it starts as a 10 you can track how quickly it goes down to a 2 or 3. Sometimes it is good not to completely remove the fear; for example a slight wariness to some spiders is natural and sensible; or maintaining a slight wariness and sensibleness of heights.

It is often best to visit a train, qualified and respectable therapist that knows how to use the rewind technique as it is best to be guided through the process rather than try to do the process to yourself.

If you know a therapist personally or know someone that knows of a therapist they can recommend then this is probably the best person to see. If not then I would recommend finding a therapist trained in Human Givens Therapy.

Addictions

We are all born with the ability to create habits and with the process to get addicted. Without these abilities mankind wouldn't have lasted as long as we have. There are many things that naturally turn into habits so that we don't have to pay all our attention to them just to do them. Like driving a car, brushing teeth etc…

Sometimes this process gets high-jacked by a negative habit, like finding yourself smoking before you realise what you are doing. The process for addiction also serves a useful purpose. The process gives you a 'high' when you do something and causes irritation or uncomfortableness when you don't.

This process is required for survival and evolution.

For example when a stone-age man used a stick to break open a coconut the 'high' of that achievement wears off over time so the stone-age man then turns that stick into an axe with a piece of flint. He then gets another 'high' from that achievement which also wears off over time. This process keeps the stone-age man reaching a point where he needs to do something to get that same high. Addictions high-jack this process giving a 'high' when carrying out the addictive behaviour and causing uncomfortableness when fighting to not carry out the behaviour. Over time you need to do more of the addictive behaviour to get the same 'high'.

A useful analogy of addiction and the associated cravings is one of a company that wants to make positive changes. The 'boss' which is the part of you that is saying 'I want to quit smoking (for example)' has good intentions. Beneath the boss is a 'secretary' that monitors incoming messages from the body. The 'security guard' monitors levels of various chemicals in the body but doesn't know what should or shouldn't be there, the guard just alerts the secretary if any of the chemicals begin to go missing or reduce.

When the boss has stopped the intake of nicotine, after a short while it starts reducing in the blood. The security guard notices this and so he emails a message to the secretary. This message is laced with dopamine which is a feel good chemical. The secretary checks on the computer and sees that the boss has said 'no cigarettes'. So the secretary ignores the message. As the nicotine goes down even further the security guard sends another message laced with even more dopamine. This time the secretary does a search on the computer for memories where nicotine has been taken into the body, and searches for memories that are also laced in dopamine. What the secretary discovers is that smoking has made the boss feel good when stressed, when bored, when socialising, etc... So the secretary sends a message to the boss laced with even more dopamine for the boss to act on.

If the boss ignores this message the secretary the process continues until eventually the boss gives in. What the 'boss' needs to do is as well as sending a message saying 'I don't want to smoke' (for example) they need to send 'memories' to link to that decision of negatives of smoking, all those things that make the boss feel bad/upset/unhealthy etc and memories linked to not smoking of feeling great/healthy/full of energy/happy etc. This way when the secretary checks the computer to find memories relating to the addiction to decide whether to keep pestering the boss or ignoring the security guard they will find these new memories instead of the 'feel good' memories that were linked to the addictive behaviour.

The more positive the 'non-addictive' memories are and the more powerful the negative 'addictive' memories are the less craving people generally have. It almost sets up a mindset of being so sure of your decision to quit that there isn't room in your thinking to have a craving.

The negative addictive behaviour may have once served a purpose

People start addictive behaviour for many reasons. It could be many things from peer pressure to experimentation. Often the behaviour initially is only in one context, like smoking with specific friends, or drinking with friends. One thing that all addictive behaviours have in common is that they give you a 'high'. It could be a 'high' from doing a risky extreme sport, or a 'high' from taking a specific substance.

To start with this addictive behaviour is in your control. The bigger the 'highs' the sooner the addictive behaviour takes on a life of its own. Due to the way the brain works at some point when you feel anxious or bored you will want to relieve this feeling. To do this you turn to the most effective thing you know, which is often the addictive behaviour. This how you begin to create a habit for that behaviour. As long as you continue to do the addictive behaviour your mind will get used to the levels of various substances in your blood stream, whether these substances are created by your mind, like endorphins, dopamine, adrenaline etc, or whether these substances are added to your blood stream like nicotine.

Once you stop the addictive behaviour it takes a period of time for the chemicals in your blood to go back to normal. This period of time can be as little as a few hours for chemicals created internally, to a few days for chemicals like nicotine and longer for some stronger drugs. Once the chemicals in the blood have normalised all that is left is the habit, not the need for the chemicals.

The reason for turning to the addictive behaviour when you feel anxious or bored is that it gives you pleasure or an instant feeling of gratification when you carry out the behaviour. Unfortunately most addictive behaviour quickly follows with a greater feeling of anxiety or depression as the effects of the behaviour wear off. This means that you have to do more of the addictive behaviour to get the same results.

Beating the addiction

To beat the addiction you need to link the addictive behaviour with the most negative outcomes you can vividly imagine, and not carrying out the addictive behaviour with the most positive outcomes that you can vividly imagine. People with addictions will always have one or more of the basic needs or essential skills not being met, so check the lists and find constructive ways to meet these.

Plan for times when you are most likely to give in to the addiction, finding ways to prevent the old behaviour pattern.

Don't be put off by a relapse. Many people have a few relapses before they finally completely get rid of that addictive behaviour. It is important to use any relapse as a lesson and see what you can learn from it. For example; what led to the relapse, how can this be avoided or prevented in the future? When the addiction strikes it is actually only mildly uncomfortable to ignore the urge for the addictive behaviour but it tricks you into thinking it is worse normally by absorbing all of your attention so that it is all you are focusing on or thinking about. It also only lasts a few minutes. Try comparing it to other things like would you prefer a severe ongoing toothache or this brief uncomfortableness for the addictive behaviour? Relax, this lets you think more objectively and clearly. To relax you could breathe in to the count of 7 and out to the count of 11. The longer out breath triggers the relaxation response. Regularly vividly imagine the negative outcomes had you continued with the addictive behaviour (doing this at the time of any cravings helps to link the negative effects with the craving as well as the act of carrying out the addictive behaviour) and vividly imagine the positive outcomes of not carrying out that behaviour, what will it be like? What are the benefits? Who else benefits? Etc…

Another option is to scramble the addictive behaviour. So for example write down the process of the addictive behaviour into stages. In individual sessions I often scramble the pattern surrounding the craving. If the person can't get the craving they are unlikely to want to carry out the addictive behaviour.

It could be that a certain amount of stress needs to build up, followed by becoming irritated, then feeling the craving coming on (perhaps a feeling in the stomach), then it reaches a critical level where you stop everything to act on it, followed by the act of carrying out the addictive behaviour, then getting a feeling of relief.

After getting the stages like this you would establish what you would like to happen instead in sensory language stating what you will be doing instead. Then take the stages of the problem, give each stage a number, and then write four columns of those numbers in different orders. Then close your eyes as you imagine the stage associated with the first number in the first column. Then open your eyes and see what the second number in that first column is, then close your eyes and imagine that stage. Do this for all the numbers in all the columns. It is important that you open your eyes between imagining each stage as this 'breaking up' of the sequence and having each part imagined separately is what breaks the old pattern. Then close your eyes and run through the ideal future behaviour that you will be doing instead. Get as absorbed in this part as you want. This way your mind has a complete pattern for the desired response and a jumbled experience of the old response making it more likely to struggle with the old response and prefer the easy option of following the complete pattern.

Sleep Difficulties

Sleep is fundamental to survival. Proper sleep boosts the immune system, refreshes and revitalises you for the following day. When you go into dream sleep the brain closes off all unfinished emotionally aroused patterns from throughout that day. Some people may think that they never dream or that they never sleep but all those people do sleep and dream. Sleeping and dreaming is so fundamental to life that without it people would die. On average people nowadays sleep for about 20% less time each night than people did a hundred years ago. This reduction in sleep has a dramatic effect on health. Sleep deprivation causes many accidents and increases the risk of psychiatric problems. Without sleep people find it increasingly difficult to function correctly, they have poorer memory and co-ordination skills etc...

Insomnia is probably the most common sleep disorder. It is often caused by excessive worrying. This can make it difficult to relax and fall asleep. It also makes you dream too much which then makes you wake up tired (see depression section). Stopping worrying during the day will often help to lift the insomnia. It will also help to stop nightmares (it also will help if you reduce anxiety-see anxiety section). Many sleep problems from night terrors (which occur in non-dream sleep and the sufferer awakens with no memory of the incident) to nightmares (bad dreams) are often due to anxiety and worrying or unexpressed thoughts from the day.

To help improve your sleep it is advisable to make sure that you don't have a clock near the bed that you can see as seeing how long you are awake for can lead to worrying about it which then makes it harder to sleep. To help you to relax and sleep at night you can purchase a relaxation CD to focus on as you go to sleep or you can learn to relax yourself.

To relax yourself you can learn to tense and relax your muscle groups from your head to your feet in time with your breathing. Tensing up as you breathe in to the count of 7 then letting the muscles relax as you breathe out to the count of 11. Then pausing briefly to get a sense of that relaxation and beginning to get an idea of a pleasant 'special place' forming in your mind that can become like a brief waiting room before you pass into sleep. After pausing you can then move onto the next muscle group (the neck for example) again breathing in to the count of 7 as you tense then out to the count of 11 as you relax, then pausing again. Doing this each night will retrain your brain to relax when it is time to go to sleep at night. Currently your brain will have been expecting the night to involve worrying or distracting thoughts etc... Some people may find that within a night or two of doing this they are sleeping properly others may take a week or a little longer before they regularly sleep well throughout the night.

Some tips to have the best chance of rapidly sleeping well if you find you're in bed for a while and still not asleep then get up and go to a dark, cool room and sit there for 30minutes.

Always wake up early (don't lie in). If possible don't do shift work. Don't watch TV or use a computer within an hour of going to bed. Don't eat or drink too much within 2 hours of going to bed. Avoid alcohol, cigarettes and other substances within 3 hours of going to bed. Avoid going to bed drunk. Have a hot bath 30 minutes before going to bed. Don't exercise within 2 hours of going to bed. Another idea you can do is attempt to stay awake for an hour longer than the time you would've normally ended up falling asleep (not the time you normally would have gone to bed and whilst you are awake do something like sitting and reading a 'boring book' or doing light, non-strenuous housework etc rather than anything overly stimulating). Do this experiment to see what happens when you try to stay awake later. Many sleep problems are due to excessive worry or excessive emotional arousal. Learning to relax and be calm will help improve the quality and quantity of sleep you get.

Drinking alcohol or taking sleeping pills to help you to sleep is not advisable because they disrupt sleep patterns (unless prescribed by a Medical Doctor as a last resort). They may help you to get to sleep quicker but they disrupt sleep that goes on a few hours later. This disruption upsets the balance of rapid eye movement sleep and deep slow wave sleep. Due to receiving less rapid eye movement sleep you don't close off all of the emotional arousing patterns from the day before so you get a build up of open patterns requiring more R.E.M sleep the next night and then more the night after that etc…

This makes you feel worse during the day and be more prone to anxiety problems as your brain is already overloaded with emotional arousal. You are likely to also get very emotional very quickly at almost nothing and not know why. Deep sleep is required for healing. So with reduced deep sleep you don't do the required amount of healing on your body that you need to be doing. The deep sleep is involved in keeping your immune system charged up and in growth so both of these areas will also be affected so you may fall ill more frequently due to lowered resistance to illnesses.

Obsessive Compulsive Disorder

OCD is often linked to ritualism and addiction. It is usually to do with anxiety or insecurity (see anxiety section). The behaviour is often very ritualistic and if it is not carried out or the obsessive thought is fought against then it can cause feelings of anxiousness or uncomfortableness. Normally people with OCD have one or more of their basic needs (see basic needs section) not being met. Often needs like needing a sense of control. When these get met it will help the OCD lift.

The most common compulsions in adults are:

- Thoughts of contamination (Obsessive washing or cleaning)

- Doubt (Did you lock the doors? Etc)

- Thoughts of having physical symptoms

- Symmetry (Straightening pictures, etc)

- Aggressive thoughts

Compulsions are usually carried out to prevent or reduce anxiety or distress. Often it is believed the compulsive behaviour will prevent a nasty event occurring. OCD affects not just the person carrying out the behaviour but also those around them. When a compulsion is carried out the person enters a trance as the compulsion takes control. This trance can be triggered by specific situations, thoughts, feelings or times of the day or by a heightened level of tiredness.

To help remove the compulsion, imagine watching a screen with someone calmly NOT carrying out the compulsive behaviour. Notice what they look like, how relaxed they appear, how you know they are relaxed. Notice how well everything goes before during and after they hadn't carried out the compulsive behaviour. Notice what else is better for them as they continue to behave differently. Then take a few moments to relax deeply and gently into that person in the screen. Seeing through their eyes, hearing what they would hear. 'Try on' their behaviour and beliefs. 'Pretend' what it is like to be them. Enjoy the feelings. Notice how much calmer you feel. Notice the benefits of being this way. Go to some old familiar situations where you had carried out the compulsive behaviour and notice the difference in how you respond to those situations as this person. Notice how calm you feel, how unbullied you feel to be going through the situation being the one in control, calm and relaxed. Then imagine being this person in some future situations when you would expect to have carried out that old compulsive behaviour. Notice how pleasurable it is to respond in this more desirable way. Practice this regularly. If occasionally you still get the old compulsive feeling which can happen for a short while as you adjust to not doing that old behaviour do this experiment (or create your own variation of this that suits your specific compulsive behaviour) – each time you feel the need to carry out the compulsion treble it. E.g., if you have to check everything is locked 3 times before you leave the house then check it 9 times. Stick to this whenever you feel the need to carry out the compulsive behaviour.

The idea with this experiment is that by increasing the compulsion you are taking control of it because you are now choosing to do it rather than having it control you. The reason for doing more of it rather than less is because it is easier to do more of something you struggle to stop rather than less. The effect of taking control of the behaviour is that it stops it being automatic which gradually stops it happening uncontrollably in the future.

So when you create your own variation of this experiment you don't want to make it easy and comfortable by just choosing to do it or increasing it a little you want to overdo it. For example hand washing could double or could be washing and drying each finger in turn, then the palm of each hand in turn then repeating this ten times. Straightening things could be straightening by exactly a millimetre at a time, stepping back, looking, straightening again and if you accidently straighten by more than a millimetre at a time you start again.

Stress Management

Anger and stress related conditions are on the increase. They are damaging to your health. They lower the immune system, increase the risk of heart problems and the chances of developing cancer, and they interrupt sleep patterns affecting the quality and the quantity of the sleep. They affect relationships and increase the susceptibility to getting addictions.

Anger is useful when used to defend yourself or loved ones. It is designed to be used for a short period of time. When you get the strong emotion of anger or become stressed (which happens when a situation becomes more than you can deal with) the emotional part of the brain takes control. This then shuts down the logical part of the brain lowering your intelligence to that of a young child whilst at the same time shutting down the digestive system and releasing adrenaline into the body ready to fight or run away. The anger comes from feeling threatened and feeling the need to defend. Situations don't cause stress; your response to the situation causes the stress. The ability to objectively view situations and see multiple viewpoints is reduced by increased stress. This black and white/all or nothing thinking increases the likelihood of getting angry easily. This make you think even the slightest disagreement or 'wrong look' is an attack, which needs defending.

The most effective way to deal with stress is to learn to relax. Use relaxation techniques like guided imagery. Create a pleasant place in your mind that you can go to whenever you need to relax. To relax get used to breathing in to the count of 7 & out to the count of 11. This releases chemicals into your blood that causes relaxation. Take a few moments to work out what is under your control. If it's not under your control there is no point worrying about it as there is nothing you can do.

Learn to problem solve rather than worry. Think 'what can I do to resolve this?' Get used to what your triggers are that caused stress or anger. Vividly imagine being in those situations and responding calmly & rationally then practice in your mind responding to similar and tougher situations in the future. By doing this you train your mind to respond in this more productive way.

Low self-esteem, lack of confidence

Low self esteem and self confidence is something that many people claim to suffer with. Even though many people say that they lack confidence, really this term is too vague. Everybody lacks confidence in certain areas of their lives. To be confident you need to know what you are doing. If you don't know how to drive you wouldn't be confident in your ability to safely drive a car across town.

When you think about whether you lack confidence, think about how you know that. What you will find is that you will lack confidence only in certain areas of your life. You are likely to be confident that the sun will rise in the morning; you are likely to be confident that the floor will be beneath you when you get out of bed in the morning. To have confidence you need to have competence at what you are doing.

Low self-esteem comes from not feeling good about yourself. This could be about your image, or about your abilities. It is really a judgement made by you about yourself. Many people with low self-esteem often get pushed around and bullied. They will feel worthless and feel that things are always out of their control.

To help increase confidence look at what you know and what you feel you need to learn to make you confident of your abilities. When someone isn't confident public speaking, for example, it is often because they haven't done it before, or have only done it a few times in the past or because they don't know the material fully enough that they will be having to talk about. There is a difference between lacking confidence at public speaking and so feeling anxious and having a phobia for public speaking. Lacking confidence and getting too anxious can cause the speaker to develop a phobia but a phobia and a lack of confidence are two different things.

Ask yourself how you know that you lack confidence, what areas of your life do you lack confidence and are these areas related in anyway. For example, it could be that you lack confidence public speaking and lack confidence when you are at parties and so feel you couldn't approach people to talk to. Both of these may be related by the fact that they both involve talking to strangers. You could test this by imagining situations to see if this seems plausible. By doing this you can work out what you really lack confidence in rather than thinking that you lack confidence in many areas of your life.

I remember someone having a fear of flying and a fear of travelling on trains. It turned out they had a fear of being trapped on something with no immediate way off if they panicked. This was what we resolved and it cleared up many other issues. The same applies for confidence. If you find out what the similarities are between all areas of lacking confidence and test your ideas you can then make sure you are dealing with a 'cause' or 'root issue' rather than just a small part of it or just a symptom of something more.

After you have done this you can think of things you are confident about. Once you have thought of a few different things, stand up; make sure you have plenty of space around you. Close your eyes and imagine seeing a confident you standing in front of you doing something that, that you is confident doing. It could be that they are confident they know how to make a cup of tea, or they are confident they can shower correctly. Just watch them confidently carrying out that behaviour. Then have them go back to the beginning of that behaviour and notice how you know that they are being confident. How do they stand, talk, etc... Now step into them and feel what it feels like to have their confidence. Hear their confident voice in your mind, behave in their confident manner. Spend some time in their confident situations standing in their place and with your eyes closed imagining going through experiences they find they are confident in.

Next imagine seeing someone you know is confident in situations you don't feel confident in. It could be a colleague, friend, film star. Whomever it is just imagine they are standing in front of you carrying out that behaviour confidently. Watch them and see what you can notice that makes you think they are so confident. Watch them in past situations that you didn't feel confident in. See what they do differently and how things go for them when they go through those situations. Watch them in many past situations that you didn't feel confident in. Then step into that person in front of you and experience what it is like to be them in those situations that previously you weren't confident in. see through their eyes, hear what they would hear and feel what they would feel. Go through as many past situations as you can think of experiencing what it is like to be this person in those situations. Notice how things are different, notice what reaction this person gets in those situations, notice what changes in those situations. Be as observant as you can. Take your time to do this in depth.

Once you have done that go back through the situations and imagine as this person, each situation and what the future consequences are. What changes occur because this person acts differently in those old situations. Take your time again to do this fully.

Now staying as you are, see that person in front of you, watch them in future situations that you would have lacked confidence in. notice as much as you can that lets you know that they are confident in those situations. Again take your time when doing this. See them in as many anticipated situations as you can think of.

Now step into that person in front of you and become absorbed in being them. See what they would see, hear what they would hear and feel what they would feel. Go through all of those anticipated situations as that person, experience what it is like to be them, notice how the situations are different to how they would normally have been expected to go. Take your time. Allow yourself to become absorbed in the experience. Once you have been through as many anticipated future situations as you can think of, then imagine some of these again, only this time imagine the future outcomes of behaving in this new way in those situations. Notice what benefits there are to being more confident. Continue to take your time.

Now imagine seeing yourself in front of you. Seeing a confident you. Watch that you responding in a new confident way in many anticipated situations. Notice what it feels like to see yourself being so confident. Notice how people are responding to this new you. Once you have watched yourself experience many anticipated situations that you previously would have lacked confidence step forward into that new improved you, that confident you. Experience those anticipated situations as this confident you, seeing what you would see, hearing what you would hear, and feeling what you would feel. Take your time to enjoy this experience. Once you have done this hold onto this feeling of confidence by clenching your fist gently. Now whilst holding onto this feeling of confidence step back a few paces to where you were in the present when you first closed your eyes. Once you are back to the present position release the fist and open your eyes. Now close your eyes and close your fist gently and allow the feeling of confidence to come back to you. Spend a few moments thinking about an upcoming situation where you want this confidence and experience having this confidence as you go through that situation, seeing what you will see, hearing what you will hear and feeling what you will feel.

It can be useful to have someone with you to help you through the above confidence building process.

Often people that lack confidence or have low self-esteem have a voice inside their mind that tells them negative things. This voice is often not a very pleasant sounding voice. It says things like, 'you are so ugly', 'you're going to mess everything up', 'everyone hates you'. What you need to do with the voice is to write down the main things that the voice says in your mind. Then go through each sentence and hear that voice speaking in a Mickey Mouse voice, then hear it speaking in a slooooow boooooooring drooooone, then hear it speaking to you in the sexiest, most seductive voice you can imagine. What you want to do is to take control away from the voice and know that you are in control. You can make it sound how you want it to sound. Pick a voice that when you hear it you can't take it seriously, perhaps it makes you laugh or it seems ridiculous. Imagine a volume control in your mind that you can turn down. Enjoy playing around with the voice, imagine it saying everything backwards. This will all help to stop that voice having power in the future.

To increase self-esteem you need to increase your opinion about yourself. Ask yourself how you know you have low self-esteem. Write these reasons down. Now ask yourself how you would be if you didn't have low self-esteem, how would you know. Answer these positively write what would be different not what you wouldn't be doing. For example, rather than writing 'I wouldn't be embarrassed in front of people' write 'I would stand tall, make eye contact, smile, etc...'

Your mind achieves what it focuses on. So if you think about what wouldn't happen, that is what will happen. For example, if I said don't think of a pink elephant, you will think of a pink elephant. If I said think of a red horse, you would think of a red horse and so NOT be thinking of a pink elephant.

Now with each point on your list of how you would be different if you didn't have low self-esteem and how you would know, go through the process above that was used for confidence and use that process for each point on your list. It can help to get someone to go through the above process with you.

As well as doing the process above write down as many good points about yourself as possible that are undeniably true. Again write these down positively. So rather than writing, 'I have got no wrinkles' write 'my face has a smooth clear complexion'. Do this regularly.

Finally for self-esteem, stand up in a room with space around you. Think of someone that loves you. If you can't think of anyone think of someone you know likes or respects you. Sometimes I get a few clients that will still tell me they can't think of anyone. If you still can't think of anyone then think of someone from your past that you know loved you. Now imagine standing in front of that person facing each other. As you look at them, get a sense of how you know they love you. Now step to the right and turn to face both you in the position you have stepped from and the person that loves you. Notice from this position how you know that the loving person loves you. Now step into the loving person and see through their eyes looking at you. Feel what they feel towards you. Notice from this position how you know you love that person in front of you. Now hold onto that feeling of love and allow your fist to gently close, take a few relaxing breaths as you feel the love grow. Then release the fist for a few seconds, then close the fist again gently and notice the feeling increase, then release the fist again. Then step back into that you in the position you started in. And imagine as you step back into yourself that as you turn to face the direction you were facing to start with, that a mirror is facing you so that you see yourself in front of you. Now as you look at yourself allow the fist to close gently and feel the love grow and notice how with the power of your breathing gently and slowly you can release that fist whilst holding onto that feeling of love for the person in the mirror.

Now open your eyes when you are done and go to a real mirror and spend time practicing holding onto that love whilst looking at yourself.

To keep a raised self-esteem it is important to check the basic needs list to ensure that all the needs are being met healthily. If any aren't then work on finding ways to meet those needs. Some people lack self-esteem or confidence because they have unrealistic expectations and believe too much is in their control. Check this out also. Think about what you expect and whether things really are within your control. If something isn't in your control then relax and let the control rest in the appropriate places. One of the most important essential skills is to accept that the only certainty in life is uncertainty. Remember you don't have to know everything perfectly before doing things. Not everything is black and white, notice the greys. If you make mistakes you learn lessons. Every entrepreneur says that mistakes are vital to success. If babies quit or didn't try things for fear of making mistakes then no baby would ever learn to walk or talk. Babies fall down hundreds of times before they can finally walk.

Pain management

There are three different components to pain. There is future anticipated pain, that is the pain you expect to experience in the future, there is past remembered pain, when you look back you remember the pain you have had, and there is the current pain in the here and now. When you experience pain it gets made worse by your knowledge of how much it hurt in the past, because you are thinking about the pain, and worsened by your anticipation for more pain to come. Some of this pain can be alleviated just by having a knowledge that the pain will end. This unfortunately doesn't happen to those with chronic pain.

It is important that pain is checked out medically. Pain is a signal. It is there for a reason. It is telling you to protect the part that hurts. In different circumstances this signal can mean different things. If you got mugged or attacked and the pain came from that it will mean, and feel different to if the pain was the result of a life saving operation or giving birth to a beautiful baby.

To begin to reduce the pain you need to know some information about it. You need to know when it is worse, and when it feels more comfortable. You need to know exactly where it hurts. When people describe pain they often generalise the area that hurts. It could just hurt on the elbow but they will say it hurts their arm. This might seem like a trivial point but if the person says that it hurts their arm then they are likely to experience more pain than if they narrow down the area to just the elbow, or to the back of the elbow. Often pain can also carry an emotional component. It can affect your basic needs. It could be that it stops you from sleeping through the night. Or it could stop you being able to do physical activities. It is important to recognise needs that need to be met because if you begin to feel low or depressed, whether independently from the pain or because of the pain, serotonin will be lower in your blood.

Serotonin reduces the pain signal, so if you are depressed pain will hurt far more. Likewise happiness, laughter and being positive increases serotonin and reducing pain and discomfort

Pain is a trance state. It focuses your full attention onto it making you very aware of how much it hurts; you then begin to describe the pain to yourself in words that have painful connotations, like sharp, stabbing, and burning. This also increases the pain.

There are many ways to reduce pain. Everyone has had an experience where they cut themselves but don't notice it straight away because they are busy, and it doesn't start to hurt until you notice it. Like when you are chopping vegetables or salad and only notice you have cut yourself and feel the pain when you see the blood.

To reduce pain you can start by renaming it perhaps as discomfort. This helps because it is a softer word and contains the word comfort which feels nice. All of these techniques and ideas work well for children as well as adults. You can grade the pain out of ten. This instantly gives the pain a boundary. You can then check as that pain lowers. Begin to describe the pain as a separate entity as if it isn't a part of you. Saying 'that pain' instead of 'the pain'.

There are a number of useful techniques involving dissociation to reduce and remove pain. One good way to dissociate is to visualise the pain. Visualise where it is and what it might look like, what colour it would be, what shape, what size. Imagine moving that image to another place, then imagine changing the shape of it, changing its colour to a colour you find calming, imagine shrinking it down and imagine moving it outside of your body and watching it move further away and being trapped somewhere, perhaps in a room or falling to the floor and rolling away or falling down a drain.

Another visualisation technique is to imagine a bright white light that wraps around the pain and shrinks down to smaller than a pea, then moves outside of your body, falls to the floor and rolls away. A useful visualisation technique for migraines is to imagine the size, shape, colour and texture of the pain. Then imagine smoothing out that shape and imagine cutting a corner off of the shape. Then tilt your head so that the liquid inside the shape can fall out from the cut corner. Once all of the liquid has fallen out you can imagine rolling the shape up to squeeze out the last of the liquid like squeezing out the last of the toothpaste in a tube. Then imagine what is left dissolving and relaxing your muscles in your head and all the blood vessels.

If the pain is caused from eating ice cream or other cold food then lick the roof of your mouth with your tongue. The reason for this is that when you eat cold food it makes the blood vessels that run along the roof of your mouth and up to your brain constrict. This causes a headache. If you lick the roof of your mouth you warm up the vessels and quickly get pain relief.

Sometimes it is useful to keep a sensation in place of the pain. It could be a tingling or another sensation. This can be useful with pain associated with pregnancy when it is important to maintain awareness for the life growing inside of you. You can use similar techniques to those described above just replacing the pain with another sensation. You can use self-hypnosis to practice. Sometimes it can be useful to use self-hypnosis to practice this if you want to reduce the actual pain of child birth. If you are doing this make sure that you tell yourself that if there are any complications during birth your body can give you a sign by changing the feeling back to pain. You can also use the self-hypnosis to mentally rehearse the child birth going comfortably.

My favourite form of pain control is to pretend to take strong pain killers. This works because your brain operates by pattern matching. If it has taken pain killers that work well in the past it will remember how those pain killers work. If you can carry out enough of the pattern to trigger the unconscious process it will give you the same relief as the real tablets. For example, imagine putting the tablets into your hand. Imagine putting those tablets into your mouth and swallowing them down with water. Then just wait for them to start working. The advantages to this approach are that if you need more relief you can take a few more imaginary pills. I find this technique easy to do and highly effective. It works similar to placebos (fake medication the recipient believes is real).

Daydreaming For Success

When I looked at highly successful people in their chosen fields from Entrepreneurs like Richard Branson & Peter Jones to Geniuses like Albert Einstein & Leonardo Da Vinci, and creative people like Beethoven & Walt Disney I discovered that they all had one thing in common. They all spent time daydreaming about their area of success.

For example:

"When I get an idea I start at once building it up in my imagination." **Nikola Tesla**

"When I heard the music it made pictures in my head...here are the pictures." **Walt Disney (Describing the film Fantasia)**

"I...go over again in the imagination the main outlines of the forms previously studied, or of other noteworthy things conceived by ingenious speculation; and this exercise is entirely to be commended, and it is useful in fixing things in the memory." **Leonardo Da Vinci**

"I would sit in my father's office chair and pretend I was in charge of a big company – a big dream for a school boy but one that ultimately came true...I believe a vibrant imagination is the lifeblood of a successful entrepreneur." **Peter Jones (From his book 'Tycoon')**

Every person I looked at had daydreaming as a part of their strategy for success. I discovered that you really do seem to get what you spend most of your time dreaming about.

From this discovery I began to look further into research on dreaming. I found that dreaming enhances creativity, updates patterns in the mind (retention of new information) and bypasses the critical factor (so that you don't question the likelihood of what is happening in the dream, you just go with it).

These discoveries led to my understanding of what makes daydreaming so important for success.

When you daydream anything is possible and unlike night-time dreaming there is a greater sense of malleability (often in night-time dreaming you just experience it without control unless you can 'lucid dream'). You can slow down or speed up time, zoom in or out, be associated or disassociated, add or take away what you like, alter the laws of physics, and so much more. As dreaming updates patterns in the mind what you dream about becomes a part of who you are. Dream of being successful and you're likely to become successful.

I discovered that how you dream is important. It isn't about just dreaming once, it needs to be so compelling that you can't stop yourself dreaming about what you want to achieve until you have got it. It has to motivate you into action.

I found that these dreams take a specific form. Firstly the BIG dream; what do you REALLY want. Then dreaming how you will get there or what the stages are, followed by frequent dreams of the bigger picture and what you need to do over the next few stages towards success. This pattern of dreaming leads to increased motivation and an increase in 'luck' or opportunities.

Part of becoming successful is to be able to learn a chosen subject successfully. For successful learning I found that people need the opportunity to daydream about what they are being taught.

Sports Psychologists use visualisation. Studies have shown that those that use visualisation outperform those that use practice alone.

Teachers tell pupils off for not paying attention or daydreaming in class; they should instead be encouraging and facilitating daydreaming. As long as the daydreaming is related to the subject rather than to something like 'what will I be doing later' the pupil will be updating patterns in their mind adding the new learning to what they already know.

I discovered a number of ways to encourage this daydreaming. I found that once something has been taught the mind needs to update the patterns within about 20 minutes; and it takes about 10 to 20 minutes for this updating to be completed.

If you take longer than twenty minutes before starting to update the patterns much of what was learnt has drifted from the mind. It will still be there somewhere but it would now be very difficult to recall it (unless it has strong emotion attached to it).

Ways to encourage this updating include:

- Using relaxation and pleasant guided imagery (this stimulates a daydream state when done correctly)

- Allowing the person to doodle (as they doodle they drift into a daydream state)

- Facilitating natural daydreaming (allowing it to happen when it is observed)

To help you to achieve success you can use the 'Six Step Success Plan'

Before I show you the 'Six Step Success Plan' here is a collection of some more people that have, or do use dreaming to achieve their success:

"I imagine a vast web of possible future paths in my head, like trails on map. I mentally explore paths that catch my interest. After I find the ones that motivate me, I revisit them often and get fascinated about what would have to happen and who I'd have to become to make it real. Then I wonder how great all of that would feel, where I could start, how proud of myself I'll be for starting, then I realize that these very thoughts are the beginning and I then get awestruck and delighted by the elegance of the universe and get cracking." **Jamie Combs (American Entrepreneur; Founder of 'Natural Balance Foods')**

"I wake from dreams and go, 'Wow put this down on paper.'...I feel somewhere some place it's been done and I'm just a courier bringing it into the world." **Michael Jackson**

Paul McCartney *dreamt he heard the Rolling Stones performing a song. When he woke up he realised the song didn't exist so he wrote it down and recorded it. The song was 'Yesterday'*

Einstein *imagined travelling on a beam of light and work with his various imaginings to create his theory of relativity.*

The story of **Newton** *was that he was relaxing under a tree when he saw an apple fall to the ground giving him his moment of understanding about gravity.*

The story of **Archimedes** *was that while relaxing in a bath he became aware that the water that overflowed as he got in could be the same as the mass of his body.*

The Six Step Success Plan

This Six Step Success Plan can be used in a variety of situations. The idea behind it is to have a technique that helps to structure your thinking.

Daydreaming is a highly effective way of creating ideas, focus and motivation. The problem is that most people struggle with spontaneous useful daydreaming.

The Six Step Success Plan involves conscious processes that make you drift inside and daydream for short periods of time as you build up ideas in sensory rich language and descriptions (which can only be got if you daydream).

Through the stages you are writing things down so that there is a conscious element that you can see in reality and use as a guide, and the unconscious element of daydreaming the various stages. The more involved and absorbed you can get in the process the more successful you are likely to be.

The final stage is to make a guided meditation that when listened to allows your mind to follow along easily and effortlessly in a daydreaming state 'fixing' what you want to achieve and the main markers on the way to that success in your unconscious mind.

It isn't enough to just dream. The dream needs to be enough to compel you to action. Through this process you have a greater chance of feeling compelled to take action and achieve success.

Stage one; make goals realistic and achievable.

For a goal to stand any chance of success you need to be in control of it. If you say you want to win the lottery you are likely to fail. If you say you want to make a million pounds by 2010 you are more likely to succeed.

Also it is important that everything you write is positive saying what you want not what you don't want (so you don't want to write 'don't each chocolate' you want to put what you want instead of eating chocolate)

You can start with a challenge, then as you explore your goal over the next few steps you can work out what is really possible. I often set very challenging goals then go through this process to see how realistic and possible they are. I allow them to be 'possible at a push' so that I really have to put in effort to achieve them.

So the first step is just to come up with what you want and write it down.

The second stage is to write the goal down giving the exact date you want to achieve it by (write it at the bottom or to the right of a piece of paper). Looking at this goal it may seem a million miles off and very unlikely and impossible. Now is when you begin to make it reality.

The third stage uses a natural talent your brain has. That is the NEED to fulfil patterns. Have you ever watched a TV programme that ends on a cliff hanger and you just HAVE to know what happens next; or read a real page turner of a book. These all use this natural ability you have to NEED patterns completed. Another natural talent is that the mind has to generalise; delete and distort information so that it doesn't get overloaded. All the information goes in but only a small percentage of it gets dripped into conscious awareness. Your unconscious mind decides what it thinks is important to you to be aware of based on other things you spend your time thinking about. For example; have you ever heard about a company that you hadn't been aware of before only to suddenly see they have vans everywhere.

With this stage you want to create a pattern for your mind to focus on and have a NEED to complete.

Start by writing down key stages between now and your ultimate goal. It really pays off in the long term to take time to do this stage. Write down what the last few stages will be just before you have achieved your goal. Ask yourself 'What do I have to do to make that possible?' as a way of working from your goal all the way back to the present. Other questions may be 'Who would you have to meet?' 'What situations will you need to get into? (Like specific social situations)' If you set a goal but then do the same as you've always done you'll get the same as you've always got. The more vivid and detailed you can make each stage the more compelling it can become. Write as many stages as you can think of.

Once you have all these stages add dates to them. This is where you may find that it could take longer than expected or it may be quicker and simpler than expected. Feel free to adjust the goal as you wish. It maybe that on paper it will take 18 months to make a million and you may want that in a year. You could either change the goal or keep the goal as one possibility knowing you will do your best to achieve the goal quicker.

Stage four you will need another sheet of paper. Write down a description of your life 'as if' you have achieved your goal. What will it be like, who will be around, what will they say, what will they notice, what will you see, hear, feel, be as descriptive as possible. This is where you find out whether this is the life you want.

Stage five is the stage where you begin to make your dreams firmly fixed in reality. In this stage you need to go through your diary placing all the dates and events you have come up with throughout the year.

A few years back I decided to do some 'home study' courses. I could do these in my own time so I had to be self motivated. The only way to remain motivated was to create my own timetable so that it was in a diary and if anyone asked if I was free I could look in my diary see that I had a 'lesson' at that time so I could say I was busy with the lesson. I made my goals as important as other diary entries.

The final stage; stage six; is the stage where you programme your mind for future success and achievement of your goals. Because you will have written everything down previously this stage is easy to do. It is the most important stage as it is the stage that will fix your goals in your mind in a way that will make your mind feel compelled to complete the patterns and achieve your dreams.

By doing this stage fully; you begin to make the goal achievement more instinctive and more a part of whom you are as a person.

In this stage you are going to make your own success achievement audio track. To do this; sit down comfortably with an audio recording device; then just talk into it 'as if' you are talking to someone else about them (so you are talking in the 'third person' saying things like 'you....' rather than 'I...').

Start by saying:

'Now as you close your eyes and relax you can listen to me and let your mind wander; and as your mind wanders you can integrate everything I say fully and honestly or discover in the future that everything I said became an integral part of who you become, and you can fall asleep while you integrate what I say or you can stay awake as you listen and absorb what I am saying to you...**(pause for about 15 seconds)**...Now talking to you in the future as someone that has achieved what you wanted I'm going to recap what you say your life is now like **(then read what you wrote for stage four in present tense 'as if' it is the current reality)** ...and I understand that you got where you are today by putting in time and effort and dedication and commitment...and that it all started when you set your mind to it back in **(add the month/year you set the goal initially)** and that you then...**(Then describe in as much detail as possible (including dates/times etc) everything you have written from the very first thing you need to do all the way through to actually achieving the goal. Read it as if it has already happened and is being recalled.**

For example: ...wrote a list of people you needed to contact back in January 2011 and in February 2011 you contacted the people on the list and arranged to meet with those that responded...etc...)'

Once you have read all of the stages end with:

'And now you are here in the future aware of the events that have passed knowing that you can drift back to the present, to the place on that journey you know you are currently at being aware of all that has passed and aware there is more yet to come, having knowledge that the present is a gift and that the future holds many more presents for you to discover...and you can relax in the knowledge that each time you listen to this you are one step closer to making your dreams reality and as you listen to this track more and more frequently you can become more used to listening to the voice on here...and when you are ready and comfortably back in the present I wonder whether you will open your eyes feeling refreshed and relaxed; or drift into a comfortable sleep'

Stage six works by accessing the REM (Rapid Eye Movement) state. This state is now known to be the state of mind used for laying down patterns and instinctive behaviours in the mind. Anyone that has learnt something consciously that now does it automatically without thinking has been through this process to make the learning instinctive so that it happens without thought or effort.

Some examples of the types of goals people may set and some stages they may include could be:

Weight loss

To Weigh 12 stone in July (so that would be losing 3lbs a month)

Stages: Eat healthy fruit bars as snacks (daily), take frequent breaks at specified times (daily), walk to work (daily)

Quitting Smoking

To be healthier and more relaxed (if you quit smoking but haven't stopped the 'cause' you will probably start again. So if you smoke due to boredom focus on the boredom as a goal, if it is due to stress focus on ways to relax at stressful times, if it is just habit look at alternative behaviours at these times etc...)

Stages: Take regular breaks (daily), get fresh air and do deep breathing (daily)

Become self employed

To have a successful therapy practice by August (would need to define 'successful' in detail)

To have 2 weekend courses running a month and 8 clients a week.

Stages: Write a business plan (January), Write a cash flow forecast (January), Put together a marketing plan (January), contact local papers and radio with a story (January)

Finally

The idea behind this book has been to write something that you can dip in and out of depending on what is going on in your life at the time. Change only happens by doing something different.

If you always do what you've always done you will always get what you've always got. I'm not here to 'make' people change or to tell people what to do. My role as a Holistic Wellbeing Coach is to facilitate people's own journey of self exploration and self expression of how they can achieve the life they want.

Everyone is unique and individual. Our greatest similarity is that we are all different and this is our greatest strength. The ideas in this book are designed to stimulate thinking without being too directive. There are some processes that are helpful to use but I hope readers will adapt things to suit themselves and to take some ownership of their own natural potentials. For example in the phobia chapter I discuss the rewind technique. With clients I rarely use the technique how it is laid out I create a version of the technique that is individual to that client. It will use the principles that make the technique work but will use what the client brings to therapy as a being with beliefs, values, interests and thought processes.

What I have learnt since I began studying the mind almost 20 years ago is that there are some fundamental aspects to living life that create happiness and wellbeing within ourselves and help us to touch the lives of others. One of these is to live life with a sense of compassion, kindness and wonder.

Every time you meet someone be curious how you can enrich their life in some way no matter how small and without desire for recognition or acknowledgement. It could be with a simple honest compliment or smile or act of kindness.

See good in others and hold on to the idea of forgiving but not forgetting. Letting go and forgiving is a very freeing act.

By not forgetting you learn from past experiences but don't hold grudges or negative judgements about people.

Show real honest curiosity when people are talking with you. Almost like a child have a desire to ask questions and be interested in what others have to say rather than interested in when you can say what you want to say. The best people to meet are those that make you feel you are interesting rather than just thinking 'aren't they interesting' or in some cases feeling inferior because the person seemed so intelligent etc.

The other fundamental aspect I have found is to have true honest self expression. We are all individuals and unique. Be yourself not what others want you to be. Many people put blocks up like thinking 'my Dad used to hit me when I did that so now I can't stand up to people' or 'That's not how it's supposed to be done so I can't do it that way'.

Elvis Presley failed music because he didn't do things 'right', Bruce Lee was constantly criticised for not sticking to just one martial art and doing things one way but instead doing 'what worked for him, for his physique, fitness, build etc'

The same holds true for overcoming problems. Everyone does things their own way. There isn't a 'one-size fits all' technique. There are some principles that work but beyond that people do things their own way. Some people approach situations head on, others find this too challenging so would rather take it slow and make small changes. Some people go cold turkey to quit addictions; others wean themselves off from addictions. Some people overcome phobias by facing the fear and just going for it. Others prefer to face it in small stages.

Hopefully you will have found information here that encourages self discovery and further exploration about certain ideas and a reflective mindset looking at yourself to see who you are as an individual and how you would like to be and what would be the best way for you to achieve that.

Made in the USA
Lexington, KY
13 February 2012